Theo in the Garden

Curiosity can grow into faith when we seek to know God.

Written by Kelsi Dykes
Illustrated by Suzi Devlin

"Ask, and it will be given to you; seek, and you will find; knock, and it will be opened to you." -Matthew 7:7

Copyright © 2025 Kelsi Dykes
No part of this publication can be reproduced without the permission of the publisher.

Published by Faith Sprouts Publishing
Pace, Florida
www.theointhegarden.com

Scripture quotations are taken from the Christian Standard Bible®, Copyright © 2017 by Holman Bible Publishers.
Used by permission. All rights reserved.

Written by Kelsi Dykes
Illustrated by Suzi Devlin
Printed in the United States of America
ISBN 979-8-218-85727-1

*For my children whose endless questions
and wonder inspire me every day, and whose hearts
I pray will always know the Lord.*

*And for every child and grown-up who reads this book,
may it spark curiosity and lead you closer to Him.*

In a quiet corner of a wild meadow lived a
curious little rabbit named Theo.
He had long ears and big, wondering eyes.
Theo loved the sound of wind in the grass,
the smell of clover after rain, and the thrill of
chasing butterflies just to see where they'd go.

But today, he found something new.
Just ahead was a garden, wild and wonderful.
Theo felt a tug in his heart,
like a question without words.

He had to see more.

Theo followed a sweet smell to a towering rose bush.
Its bright blooms reached for the sky,
like they were smiling at the sun.
He leaned to take a sniff.

"Would you like to hear a story?"
Theo blinked, thinking the flower had spoken.
He hopped closer.
On a leaf sat a ladybug. Her eyes twinkled.
"Hello!" he said. "I would love to hear a story!"

So the ladybug began:
"Once, a little lamb wandered far from her flock. The shepherd noticed right away. Even though he had ninety-nine others, he left them to find the one who was lost. He climbed hills, crossed brambles, and searched until he heard her cry. Then he scooped her up, held her close, and carried her all the way home."

"That," the ladybug said gently, "is love: kind and patient. It keeps going and it never runs out. It's the kind of love God has for us."

"God?" Theo whispered.
"Yes," she said. "He made this garden…
and you. His love is big and forever."

Theo imagined being scooped up in a big hug like the little lamb. He felt the same tug in his heart that had brought him to the garden.

"So that's what love feels like," he said softly.

Hopping farther along, Theo discovered a patch of tall sunflowers. Each turned its golden face to follow the sun. Below their leafy stems among streams of sunbeams, a chipmunk twirled and giggled.

Theo tilted his head. "Why are you dancing?"
The chipmunk grinned. "Because I found it!"
Theo wiggled his ears. "Found what?"
"My favorite button! I thought it was gone forever.
But I looked and looked—and there it was!"
Theo smiled even though he didn't quite understand.

"Jesus once told a story like this," explained the chipmunk. "A woman lost her coin. When she found it, she called all her neighbors and said, 'Come celebrate with me!'

"That's joy," the chipmunk said, doing a giant spin. "It fills your heart when something wonderful happens, like getting a hug from someone you love or finding something special you lost."

Theo didn't have a favorite button, but he hopped happily and danced with the chipmunk before continuing on his way.

Eventually, Theo wandered deeper into the garden.
A patch of soft lavender swayed gently.
He nestled beside it and closed his eyes.
The breeze slowed and every leaf and petal grew still.

"Are you asleep?" came a voice through the stillness.
Theo peeked open an eye. A turtle sat on a mossy rock. His eyes were kind and calm.

"I'm just resting," said Theo.
The turtle smiled. "Quiet moments like this remind me of a story…"

"There was a great storm.
Waves crashed, and the boat rocked wildly.
The people in the boat were afraid.

But Jesus stood up and said, 'Peace. Be still!'
And just like that, the storm stopped."
Theo opened his eyes.
The turtle was still smiling.

"Jesus didn't just stop the storm," he said, "He helped the people feel safe again. That's peace—when your heart feels calm because you know Jesus is with you." Theo breathed in the lavender-scented air. All he felt was peace.

After a while, he rose and continued down the path, his heart quiet and full.

Just as he rounded a bend,
Theo spotted a tiny fig tree.
Beneath it, a snail crawled, gazing up at a
single green fig. Theo was curious.
"Excuse me. Are you waiting for it to ripen?"
Very slowly, the snail nodded.
"It's not ready yet. But it will be."

Theo's nose twitched.
"Do you ever get tired of waiting?"
"Sometimes," said the snail,
"but good things take time."

"Jesus once told a story about a seed. It grew slowly, little by little: first a sprout, then a stem, finally a plant ready for harvest.

We don't always see something growing, but it's happening."

The snail's eyes twinkled.
"That's patience—trusting that something good is coming, even when it feels slow."

Theo lay down beside the snail,
his eyes on the fig.
He could almost taste it... but he could wait.

Theo wandered deeper into the garden, following the gentle rustle of leaves in the wind.

A patch of sweet pea vines clung tightly along the garden wall, their pink and purple blossoms tangled together, swaying in the breeze.

Buzz! Theo followed the sound.
A bee lay on the ground, its wing crumpled.
Before he could help, a squirrel dropped from a nearby tree and scooped up the bee.

She gently wrapped its wing in a soft flower petal.
Then the squirrel stayed until the bee felt better.
"Did you come just to help?"
Theo asked, wide-eyed.

The squirrel smiled. "Yes. Jesus teaches us to help those in need. Once he told a story about a hurt man. Many people passed by, but only one person stopped to help. That's kindness — stopping to care for others when they need it."

Theo thought for a moment. He picked a large leaf and carefully held it over the bee for shade.
"If kindness means showing love to others like Jesus did. I can do that!" Theo smiled brightly.

As Theo continued his journey through the garden, he found a cool, shady nook. There, soft ferns curled around the mossy ground.

A deer stepped gracefully from behind the trees. Her calm eyes glowed in the soft light.
"Hello, little one," said the deer. "You've found the part of the garden where goodness grows."
Theo looked around, his eyes wide.
"It's so quiet here," he said.

The deer smiled.
"That's what goodness is like, quiet but strong."
Theo thought for a moment.
"But how do you know if something is truly good?"

She stepped closer, her voice gentle.
"Jesus once told a story. He said, 'A good tree bears good fruit, and a bad tree bears bad fruit. A tree is known by the fruit it grows.'"
She moved toward a fern,
its soft fronds swaying in the breeze.

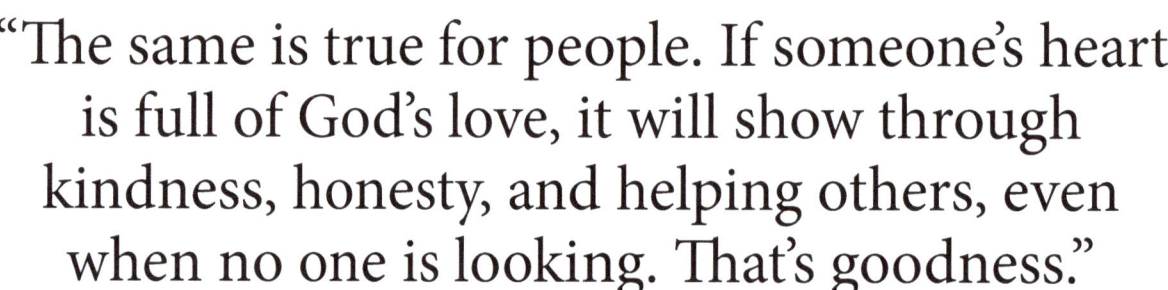

"The same is true for people. If someone's heart is full of God's love, it will show through kindness, honesty, and helping others, even when no one is looking. That's goodness."

Theo's eyes lit up.
"So, if I let God's love grow in my heart, others will see me grow in goodness too?"

The deer nodded, her gaze full of warmth.

Theo strolled along a narrow path.
Rows of leafy vines stretched far and wide.
A sweet aroma filled the air.

"Hi there!" a friendly voice called.
A plump hedgehog smiled at him.
"Hello!" said Theo.
"Do you know what grows here? It smells so good!"
"You've found the vineyard!" grinned the hedgehog.
"You smell grapes. Do you know they take a long time to grow? They need sunshine and rain, but most of all—faithfulness."

"Faithfulness?" asked Theo.

The hedgehog leaned against a round stone.
"You see, the grapes must stay
connected to the vine, day after day.
That's how they grow sweet and strong."

Theo took a good look at the vine.
The hedgehog's eyes twinkled.

"Jesus said He is the vine, and we are the branches.
If we stay close to Him, we can grow good fruit—
like love, patience, and faithfulness."

"So, faithfulness means staying close to Jesus?"

"Exactly!" said the hedgehog.
"Faithfulness means showing up again and again, even when it's hard. It's trusting Jesus every day. When we do that, just like these grapes, we'll grow little by little, sweeter and stronger."

Theo took a deep breath. "I'm going to keep showing up, just like you said. I want to stay close to Jesus so I can grow steady and strong."

"And you will," said the hedgehog.
"God is always faithful to us, every day, no matter what. He never leaves. Just keep walking with Him!"

Theo hopped along the winding path. Rows of vines faded behind him. He thought about how the vines had to grow slowly and patiently, through sunshine and storms.

"A garden must be strong to grow," he whispered.
He looked down at his little paws.

"Maybe I'm growing, too!"

Ahead, the path curved.
Soft green branches swayed gently in the breeze.
A peaceful stillness lingered in the air,
whispering through the wispy branches.
Theo stood still, gazing at the willows.

A butterfly glided by and landed on a nearby branch. "Isn't it lovely? This is the grove where gentleness grows. Gentleness is soft and thoughtful."
Theo nestled down on a patch of comfy moss and listened.

"Do you know what Jesus did when people tried to keep children away from Him?"
"No," said Theo, surprised. "What did He do?"

"He said, 'Let the little children come to Me.' He didn't turn them away. He welcomed them with open arms and held them close.
That's gentleness: strong enough to love with softness."

"So, I can be strong... and gentle?" asked Theo.
"Yes!" the butterfly smiled. "Gentleness is choosing to be calm and loving, even when you're strong. It's a strength wrapped in love!"

"Wow! That's how strong I want to be, just like Jesus!" Theo said.
He hopped up, stretched, and bounced along the path.

The evening sun cast a warm, golden light across the path. At last, Theo reached the far edge of the garden. A plum tree stood tall. Its branches drooped under the weight of tiny fruit. Some plums were soft and sweet, others were hard and green.

A wise old owl perched on one branch.
He blinked slowly in the warm sun.
"Hi there!" Theo called out, hurrying to grab the biggest and brightest plum.
The owl spoke softly, "Careful, little one. Use self-control. Not every plum is ready."

Theo paused, still reaching for the fruit. "But I really want that one. It looks so good!" The owl gave a knowing hoot. "I understand. But the sweetest fruit comes to those who wait—and those who choose wisely."

Theo pulled his paw back. "So… self-control means waiting, even if I don't want to?" "Sometimes," said the owl. "Self-control means not just going by what you feel, but choosing what you know is right. Even I must hold back, though I'm hungry too."

The owl's eyes twinkled. "Jesus helps us slow down, think, and choose what is good. That's how your heart grows the sweetest fruit of all."
Theo looked up at the tree again.
He smiled. "I think I'll choose a better one."

Night was gently approaching. Theo knew it was time to return to his meadow. He took one last look over the garden and thought about all the wonderful stories he had heard: love that never ends, kindness that changes hearts, and joy that spreads to others.

He gazed at the large, sturdy trees that stood like soldiers. "The promises in this garden… make me feel safe. And known. And wanted."

The leaves rustled in the breeze, and a familiar voice chimed in softly, "That's because they come from someone who loves you more than you can imagine."

"Jesus," Theo whispered,
a smile spreading across his face.
The chipmunk nodded, her eyes bright with kindness.

Theo studied the garden.
He placed his paws over his heart. "I want to know Him. I want Jesus to be my friend. Forever."

And in that quiet moment, the garden seemed to glow brighter. Every bloom blossomed and the breeze brought sweet smells.
Theo felt something blossom deep in his heart too—something gentle, strong, and true.
His chipmunk friend leaped with joy.

Theo knew it was Jesus. Not just a story.
Not just a name. But a friend—his friend.

He wasn't a visitor anymore.
He belonged to the garden now and to the One who made every promise come true.

Theo turned toward his meadow home
but he knew this wasn't goodbye.

Each promise he had discovered was now
tucked safely in his heart: love, joy, peace,
patience, kindness, goodness, faithfulness,
gentleness, and self-control.

These weren't promises of what Theo could
grow on his own, but of what God would
grow in Theo as he walked with Him.

And best of all, Theo now had a Friend who would never leave him. Jesus was with him. Always.

"I'll share Your promises!" whispered Theo, hopping away. "I'll help others find the way to You, too!"

With one last joyful twitch of his nose, Theo bounded into the forest, his heart full and shining. He was ready to live each day with Jesus right beside him.

www.ingramcontent.com/pod-product-compliance
Lightning Source LLC
Chambersburg PA
CBHW041413010526
44107CB00016B/1157